Module 5: Scientific Writing

Introduction

As a Science student in higher education, you need to write scientific reports of experiments and fieldwork. Your reports need to be clear enough for other scientists and readers to follow and repeat your experiments, if necessary. You will need to organise and structure your report using conventional style, language and layout. This module will help you to learn the conventions and skills required to write a good scientific report.

Unit 1 looks at how to organise your report and timetable your work up to your submission deadline. In Units 2 and 3, you will learn conventions for writing the *Method and Materials* and *Results* sections. In Unit 4, you will review conventions for writing numbers in scientific papers. Unit 5 deals with the *Discussion* section of the report, as well as the *Bibliography*, *Introduction* and *Title*. Editing and revision are essential to good writing, and you will develop these skills by doing the exercises in Unit 6.

Contents

Structure and schedule

At the end of this unit, you will learn how to:

- structure your report and include appropriate scientific report sections
- organise your time appropriately

Task 1 Organising a scientific report

When you do laboratory or fieldwork, you will be asked to write a scientific report of your experiment or investigation. Scientific papers and reports are typically divided into five sections:

1. Introduction
2. Materials and Method
3. Results
4. Discussion
5. Bibliography

Each section answers a different question. The questions answered in these sections are:

a. What do the Results *mean*?
b. What was *found/discovered*?
c. What is the *background* and *aim* of the investigation?
d. What literature *sources* are referenced in the report?
e. What was *done* in the investigation?

1.1   Complete the table to match each section (1–5) to the question it answers (a–e). Compare your completed table with your partner's.

section	question
1.	
2.	
3.	
4.	
5.	

1.2   Work as a class to discuss the reasons for your choices.

Task 2 Organising your time

When you write your report, you will not only need to write each section, but also allow time for additional research, revision and possibly discussion with your peers. You will probably have to do all this by a set deadline.

2.1 To meet deadlines, it is important to manage your time. Imagine you and your partner have to submit your reports in seven days' time. Read through the steps below and put them into a logical order. When you have finished, compare your work with your partner's.

- ☐ Revise first draft
- ☐ Write first draft of the *Introduction*
- ☐ Hand in revised draft
- ☐ Write first draft of the *Discussion*
- ☐ Write first draft of the *Materials and Methods* section
- ☐ Research background information
- ☐ Meet with another student to discuss peer review (have a writing conference)
- ☐ Start *Bibliography*
- ☐ Give first draft to another student to review, using list of 'Points to check'
- ☐ Complete practical laboratory work
- ☐ Write first draft of the *Results* (do calculations, draw up tables, graphs, charts)

2.2 Now that you have decided on a logical order of steps, think about how to time each step. Write your answers in the *activity* column of the table below and give a reason for your timing, wherever possible, in the *reason* column.

time frame	activity	reason
Day 0	Complete practical laboratory work.	
Day 1		
Day 2		
Day 3		
Day 4		
Day 5		
Day 6		
Day 7		

Note: Remember, you can adjust the time frame according to your own deadlines.

2.3 Discuss your tables in small groups. You may have your own reasons for doing things in a different way from others in the group. Give reasons for your choice.

Reflect

Construct a template you could use for writing scientific reports.

Your template should identify each of the five sections of your report, organised in the correct order.

2 The *Materials and Methods* section

At the end of this unit, you will:

- review what to include in the *Materials and Methods* section of your report
- learn how and why to write in the passive voice

Task 1 What do I include?

1.1 What question do you answer in the *Materials and Methods* section of your report?

_____

1.2 You are advised to write the *Materials and Methods* section of your report as soon as possible after completion of your practical work. Why do you think this is good advice?

_____

1.3 In the *Materials and Methods* section, you should describe how you did the experiment, writing in sufficient detail for another scientist to repeat your experiment.

Work in groups to discuss the following points. Choose a group secretary to make notes of the ideas you discuss.

a. Examples of information that should be included in a good *Materials and Methods* section, e.g., temperature, volume.

b. Examples of information that does not need to be included in a *Materials and Methods* section. (Think about your reader: what does everyone in your subject area know about the everyday equipment and techniques that you use?)

include	do not include
temperature	method for setting up a laboratory light microscope

1.4 Report back to the whole class.

1.5 Are the statements true (T), false (F), or does it depend (D)?

a. Even if well-known procedures or equipment have been used, it is necessary to describe it in detail. ☐

b. All equipment used should be listed. ☐

c. It is important to include clear references to published protocols and methods. ☐

d. The method should be explained using numbered points, as in a set of instructions. ☐

Task 2 How do I write a good *Materials and Methods* section?

You should include all appropriate information in your report. It is also important to use the most appropriate style.

> Weigh 10 g air dried 2 mm sieved soil into a 50 ml centrifuge tube. Using an automatic dispenser add 25 ml ultra pure water. Cap the tube and place on the shaker for 15 minutes.

> **pH determination**
> Ten g of soil was placed in a 50 ml centrifuge tube. Twenty-five ml of ultra pure water was added and the tube placed on a shaker for 1 hour. The pH was then measured using a calibrated pH meter.

2.1 **Complete the paragraph using the words in the box. (There are more words than gaps, so you will not need to use them all.)**

paragraphs	sentences	passive	active	imperative	past	present	future

Laboratory schedules are usually written in the _____ as a list of instructions.

However, when you write your report, you must summarise what you did in full _____ and

well-developed _____. You will usually write in the _____ tense and use the

_____ voice.

2.2 **As a class, discuss these questions about the advice in Task 2.1.**

a. Why is there a difference in grammar between laboratory schedules and reports?

b. Why is information divided up into paragraphs in a report?

c. Why is the passive voice so common in the *Materials and Methods* section of a report?

2.3 **As indicated above, the *Materials and Methods* section of your report is usually written in the passive voice. The passive is used because the procedure is more important than the person who carried it out.**

Read the sentence.

I removed the skins from the onions and homogenised them in the blender.

In a scientific report this should be written:

The onions were skinned and homogenised.

In the second sentence there is no mention of the blender. Which of the following is the most likely reason?

a. It has been mentioned in a previous part of the text. ☐

b. Only non-standard equipment should be mentioned. ☐

c. The next sentence will state: This was carried out in a blender. ☐

Task 3 Using the passive

The following two sentences describe the same event.

Active: *John conducted the analysis.* (*the analysis* is the object)

Passive: *The analysis was conducted by John.* (*the analysis* is the subject)

The analysis (or the methods, materials and procedures) is more important information for the reader than who conducted the analysis (John). The analysis is therefore usually made the grammatical subject of the sentence.

3.1 **Complete the rule.**

The object in the active sentence, *the analysis*, becomes the _____ in the passive sentence.
The subject in the active sentence, *John*, changes position in the passive sentence as it comes
_____ the main verb and is introduced with _____.

3.2 **Some verbs, such as *give*, have two objects.**

> **Active:** *We gave the caterpillars one dose every three hours.*

We can therefore choose which object we want to make the subject. We choose the one we think is most important.

> **Passive:** *The caterpillars were given one dose every three hours.*
> or
> *One dose was given to the caterpillars every three hours.*

Complete the rule.

In the active sentence above, the two objects are _____ and _____. One or the other can become the subject in the _____ sentence.

Note: Other common verbs that can have two objects are: bring, send, offer, ask, pay, lend, sell. *However, you are less likely to use these in scientific reports.*

3.3 **Read the explanation about the use of tenses, then complete the sentences.**

You write the *Materials and Methods* section of a scientific report in the <u>past</u> tense. This can be the *past simple*, the *past perfect* or the *past continuous*. Each tense works the same way in the passive – it is only the verb *to be* which changes, according to the tense chosen.

Past simple
The plant was taken.
A pot _____ made.
The image was shown.

The plants _____ taken.
The pots were made.
The images _____ _____.

Past perfect
The solution had been shaken.
The animal _____ been fed.
The mixture had been kept.

The solutions had been _____.
The animals _____ been fed.
The mixtures _____ _____ _____.

Past continuous
A record was being made.
An attachment _____ being fitted.
The result was being analysed.

Records were _____ _____.
Attachments were being fitted.
The results _____ _____ _____.

Note: In all passive sentences, to be *is singular if the subject is singular, and plural if the subject is plural.*

The box **was** being built.   The boxes **were** being built.

3.4 Read the draft of a student's *Materials and Methods* section, and the tutor's comments on it. Work in small groups to discuss what changes the student should make in response to the tutor's comments. Make notes of the points you discuss in your group.

I started my fieldwork recordings on 12 February, 2014, and ended them on 12 March, 2014. My partner used a digital camera to record the animals found on the beach and I marked the animals with quick-drying non-toxic paint. We were making recordings of environmental conditions, including the temperature, the salinity and the substrate, at the same time. I began the laboratory experiments at the same time as the fieldwork. Each day, I collected 10 animals from the beach and placed them in the controlled conditions in the laboratory until the experiments began.

We set up the apparatus as shown in Figure 1 and I placed 1 crab in each specimen tube. By the time an experiment started, we had acclimatised the crabs for at least 2 days. I had fed the crabs daily. I had prepared their food in advance. My partner used a digital camera at the end of each experiment to record the appearance of the animals. We had printed the photographs taken at the beach for comparison. We were analysing results continuously. We analysed our results using statistical tests.

Overall, you describe your methods clearly. You could improve your writing by:
- focusing the reader's attention on the method, rather than who used the methods
- paragraphing more accurately
- checking your articles (*the, a, an*)

3.5 Write the final version of the *Materials and Methods* section, using the tutor's comments and the notes you made to help you.

Reflect

The following instructions are taken from a practical class schedule. Write the *Materials and Methods* section of a scientific report of this experiment, remembering the points you have learnt in this unit.

A. Testing a leaf for the presence of starch.

- Draw your variegated leaf (taken from a geranium plant) showing the distribution of green chlorophyll.

  Your annotations should include a description of the morphology of the leaf.

- Plunge your leaf into boiling alcohol. This dissolves chlorophyll out of the leaf. Use three changes of alcohol.

  (REMEMBER: ALCOHOL IS VERY FLAMMABLE. THEREFORE, IT MUST BE HEATED IN A WATER BATH, NOT DIRECTLY OVER A FLAME.)

  SAFETY RULES: wear gloves and safety glasses; point test tube mouth away from yourself.

- Having been in alcohol, the leaf will now be brittle. Therefore, dip it into boiling water to soften it.

- Spread the leaf on a white tile. Swamp the leaf with iodine.

  SAFETY RULES: wear gloves (iodine is an irritant).

- Iodine will appear blue-black in those areas of the leaf where starch is present.

- Redraw your leaf, noting the distribution of blue-black colouration.

The *Results* section

At the end of this unit, you will:

- review what to include in the *Results* section
- learn how to present and describe tables and figures
- be able to write about your results

Task 1 What to include

1.1 **What question is answered in the *Results* section of your report?**

_____

The *Results* section of your report enables you to present your data (findings or results) to show what you found and whether it matched your expectations.

This section needs to include a short paragraph or two describing and analysing trends and results, as well as any relevant tables or figures that support your findings. It may be the shortest section of your report, but it is also the most important.

1.2 **Label the diagrams using the words in the box.**

table   histogram   pie chart   line graph

a. _____   b. _____

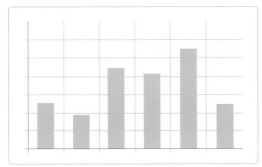

Number	Letter	Yes/No
1	F	✓
2	B	✗
3	U	✓
4	T	✓
5	S	✗
6	H	✗

c. _____   d. _____

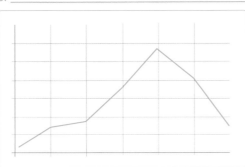

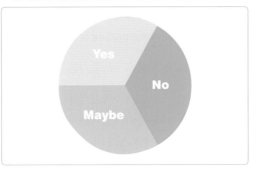

1.3 **Work with a partner to discuss the questions.**

a. What is the difference between a *table* and a *figure* in a scientific report?

b. Should the *Results* section always include tables or figures, or can the results be expressed by text alone?

c. Should the title of the figure or table be above or below it?

d. What do you think makes tables and figures easier to interpret?

Task 2 Preparing tables and graphs

If you have a large quantity of data to present, or are comparing several different things, a table can show it more clearly than a graph. Graphs and other figures, on the other hand, are a good way of illustrating and emphasising trends, particularly if they are dramatic.

Table 1: Characteristics of three populations of *Daphnia* species collected at Rye Meads Pond on 3 June, 1981

species	average length (mm)	average number of eggs	average number of animals per L
Daphnia magna	5.01	15.3	112.5
D. obtusa	2.33	8.2	68.7
D. longispina	2.77	6.8	40.4

Table 2: Characteristics of three populations of *Daphnia* species collected at Rye Meads Pond

species	*Daphnia magna*	*D. obtusa*	*D. longispina*
av. length	5.01	2.33	2.77
aver. no. of eggs	15.3	8.2	6.8
av. no. of animals	112.5	68.7	40.4

2.1 **Tables 1 and 2 present the same information, but in different formats. Discuss with a partner:**

   a. the differences between Tables 1 and 2 (think about differences in organisation, titles, the use of abbreviations, the inclusion of units)

   b. which of the tables is better organised, easier to read and makes it easier to compare results

   c. whether it is appropriate to show this information in a graph

2.2 **Work in groups to decide what features make a good table. Think about how to:**

   • show your data to make it easy to compare significant information

   • give units, arrange numbers, use abbreviations

   • give table and figure numbers, and titles

2.3 **The results below are taken from a student's laboratory notebook, and are followed by a graph (opposite) that the student made based on the data to include in a written report.**

   Discuss the strengths and weaknesses of the graph.

Temperature °C	Rate of reaction, mg. products per hr
0	0
5	0.3
10	0.5
15	0.9
20	1.4
25	2.0
30	2.7
35	3.3
40	3.6
45	3.6
50	2.3
55	0.9
60	0

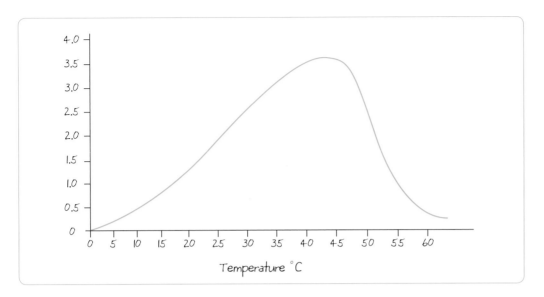

2.4 **Draw an improved version of the graph on the graph paper below.**

As you prepare your graph, you should consider the following questions:

a.   Which is the independent variable (the one that the investigator can control or manipulate)?

b.   Which is the dependent variable (the one that changes in response to the independent variable)?

c.   Are the axes organised correctly?
    Note: *The independent variable (the x-variable) is plotted on the horizontal or x-axis, and the dependent variable (the y-variable) is plotted on the vertical or y-axis.*

d.   Are the scales appropriate?
    Note: *Scales are chosen to make the plot fill the graph so that trends are easily visible.*

e.   Are the axes labelled correctly, with units?

f.   Are the data plotted accurately?
    Note: *Since the data points are measured experimentally and therefore have some inherent experimental uncertainty, it is recommended that data points are plotted with a well defined symbol. For example, the following symbols are commonly used: (●), (■), (□), (▲) or (♦). Use ONE type of symbol for ONE data set.*

g.   Are the abbreviations correct?

h.   Does the graph have a figure number and a title that enables the reader to understand what the graph represents?

i.   Is the title written below the figure?

3

Task 3 Writing the text of the *Results* section

After you have presented your results graphically, you must describe your findings in the rest of your *Results* section. As you are now describing what the results were, rather than what you did, you will usually use the past tense in the active voice.

Start with a sentence that states each important finding and which refers to the table or figure that supports this finding. Next, write about the specific details of the data shown in the figure.

3.1 Read the paragraph, taken from a *Results* section of a report, and find examples of:

    a.   use of the past tense in the active voice

    b.   a general statement describing an important finding

    c.   data that support the general statement

> Oxygen production varied depending on the pH of the solution (Figure 1). At pH 2, oxygen production was 3 ml, whereas at pH 7 it increased to a maximum of 6 ml. At pH values above 7, oxygen production decreased and was at a minimum of 1 ml at pH 10.

3.2 With a partner, discuss what points you would include in a description of the results presented in the graph you drew in Task 2. Then work individually to write a paragraph to describe the data.

3.3 When you and your partner have completed your paragraphs, evaluate each other's work.

    a.   Work in groups of 3–5. Discuss what you feel are the main features of a good description of results.

    b.   Write a checklist giving advice for writing the *Results* section.

- _____
- _____
- _____
- _____
- _____
- _____

Reflect

Take an example of a study or experiment you have carried out.

Did you present your results in the most appropriate way? Did you use tables, graphs, pie charts or text alone to present your results?

Write an improved version of your *Results* section, remembering the points you have learnt in this unit.

Writing numbers and abbreviations

At the end of this unit, you will:

* understand when to use numerals and spell numbers in scientific reports
* learn how to use very large and very small numbers
* familiarise yourself with the conventions for using abbreviations

It is essential to use numbers correctly when writing a scientific report to ensure the reader is provided with an accurate account of what happened. Even if the numbers shown in a report are correct, it is easy for the reader to be confused or overwhelmed if they are not used in a clear and conventional way.

Task 1 Writing numbers

Guidelines for writing numbers are given below. These guidelines are recommended by the Council of Science Editors (Section 12.1.2, *Scientific Style* and *Format*, 2014).

1.1 **Read the guidelines below and find an example of:**

   a.   a numeral

   b.   an ordinal

   c.   a fraction

   d.   a decimal form

1.2 **Match the five words from the guidelines (a–e) with their meaning (1–5).**

a.	adjacent	1.	exact
b.	non-quantitative	2.	worthy of attention
c.	fraction	3.	next to each other
d.	precise	4.	not a whole number
e.	significant	5.	not describing a specific amount

Numerals are used to express quantities and mathematical relationships. This makes them stand out in the text.

2 theories	7 mm
22 amino acids	0.5 nm
3 replicates	400 x magnification
378 specimens	100-fold

Situations in which numbers should be spelled out include:

When a number is at the beginning of a sentence: *Fifteen g of peas were placed in the tube.*

When two numbers are adjacent, use a numeral for the one that goes with a unit of measurement, spell out the other number: *three 25 ml samples.*

When a number has a non-quantitative meaning:

one of the specimens

was one of the most significant

the zero value

When writing ordinal numbers (numbers that convey order or rank) less than 10:

the seventh sample

a second time

When a fraction is part of the running text: *a third of the plants.*

Note: *When a precise value is required, the decimal form is used: 0.5 ml.*

1.3 **Circle the correct option to complete the sentences.**

a. Experiments lasting *one* / ①day indicated that temperature was ⓞne / *1* of the most important factors, whereas *seven* / *7* -day toxicity tests suggested that salinity was crucial.

b. *5* / *Five* gammarus were placed in *fifty* / *50* ml of *0%* / *zero per cent*, *50%* / *fifty per cent* and *100%* / *one hundred per cent* sea water solutions.

c. The animals were collected at Swansea Bay and *one half* / *$^1/_2$* / *0.5* were divided between *3* / *three* *50* / *fifty* ml pots.

d. After washing *2 times* / *twice* in buffer, the tissue was immersed in *2%* / *two per cent* osmium tetroxide in *0.25* / *.25* M phosphate buffer, for *one* / *1* hr.

Task 2 Common scientific abbreviations

Abbreviations are frequently used in scientific reports. Some abbreviations are used for technical or scientific words that occur three or more times in the text. In this case, you should define the abbreviation when you use it for the first time and put it in parentheses, e.g., Ampicillin resistant (Amp[R]). Other standard abbreviations can also be used, e.g., *ml*, *min*, and do not need to be defined.

2.1 **Write the full form of the standard abbreviations.**

a. s   _____

b. min   _____

c. h/hr   _____

d. g   _____

e. mg   _____

f. μm   _____

g. O   _____

h. MW _____

i. U   _____

j. bp   _____

k. DNA _____

l. UV   _____

Task 3 Using numbers and abbreviations in the *Results* section

3.1 Study the table, then read the extract from the *Results* section. Discuss how you could improve the features (a–e) of the table and text.

  a. arrangement of the table

  b. use and layout of numbers and units in the table

  c. abbreviations used in the table

  d. title of the table

  e. use of tenses in the text

  f. use of supporting data in the text

Table 3: Seven-day LC50 values

	D. magna		Cyclops bicuspidatus	
	cadmium (μg l^{-1})	zinc	Cd	Zn
pond A	296	5 x 10^3	3800	5.5 x 10^3
pond B	23.0	490	320	520

Table 3 shows the Seven-day LC50 values (concentrations at which half the sample dies after seven days) for cadmium and zinc for populations of *Daphnia magna* and *Cyclops bicuspidatus* collected from Pond A and from Pond B. The results indicate that for both *D. magna* and *C. bicuspidatus* the toxicity of cadmium is greater than for zinc. Animals collected from Pond B are more sensitive to cadmium and zinc poisoning than those collected from Pond A.

3.2 **Redraw the table and rewrite the text making appropriate corrections.**

Reflect

Research scientific papers published in major scientific journals, such as *Journal of Experimental Biology, Ecology* or *Nature*.

Make a note of examples of sentences, figures or tables that include:

• numerals

• numbers spelled out as words

• abbreviations

The *Discussion, Bibliography, Introduction* and *Title* sections

At the end of this unit, you will:

* review what to include in the *Discussion* section of your report
* learn how to cite references and write a *Bibliography*
* be able to write an appropriate *Introduction* and *Title*

The *Discussion* section is an important part of the report that follows on from the explanation of your methods and presentation of your results. After you have written the *Discussion*, it will be easier to organise your *Bibliography*, *Introduction* and *Title*.

Task 1 What to include in the *Discussion*

1.1 What question do you answer in the *Discussion* section of your report?

1.2 Results are interpreted and their significance is explained in the *Discussion* section of your report.

Study Table 1. It shows results for an experiment that compared the distribution of beetles in two different woodlands. Think of some questions that you might ask about the results of the experiment.

Were there any significant differences in the densities of different species of beetles counted in the two habitats?

Table 1: Mean number of beetles per quadrat for two woodlands

		mean number per quadrat	
scientific name	common name	Peasemore Wood	Hailey Wood
Aphodius nemoralis	Dung beetle	10.1	11.8
Curculio glandium	Acorn weevil	8.4	7.2
Coccinella septempunctata	7-spot ladybird	8.1	7.9
Adalia bipunctata	2-spot ladybird	6.1	5.1
Agonum assimilie	Ground beetle	4.1	4.9
Ampedus sanguinolentus	Click beetle	3.4	4.1
Byrrhus fasciatus	Banded pill beetle	3.3	3.1
Pogonocherus hispidulus	Longhorn beetle	3.2	3.1
Clytus arietus	Wasp beetle	3.0	3.0
Carabus intricatus*	Ground beetle	2.9	0
Gnorimus nobilis*	Noble chafer	2.7	0
Lucanus cervus*	Greater stag beetle	1.2	0
Ampedus rufipennis*	Click beetle	0.8	0

*Species of conservation importance

1.3 These sentences summarise the main features of the *Discussion*. Complete the sentences using the words in the box.

hypothesis	suggestions	implications	conclusions
deviations	error	general	improvements	specific

The *Discussion* section of the report will generally move from the _____ (the results of your experiment) to the _____ (how your results fit in with other scientific findings).

Normally, the discussion should do the following:

• Explain whether your results support your original _____.

• Consider any surprising data or _____ from what you expected.

• Consider sources of _____.

• Consider _____ in experimental method.

• Relate your findings to previous results in the same area and derive _____ about the process you are studying.

• Look at the practical and theoretical _____ of your findings.

• Make _____ for extensions of your study.

1.4 Read the discussion of the results shown in Table 1.

a. Which elements listed in Task 1.3 are included in this *Discussion*?

b. Underline the sentences that correspond to these elements.

Discussion

The results show that populations of common beetle species were similar in both woodlands and were comparable to numbers found in previous studies. These common beetles are found in most woodland habitats. As expected, it was also found that the diversity of beetle species was higher in Peasemore Wood than in Hailey Wood. Peasemore Wood was found to contain a high number of beetle species which are rare in the UK.

The results show that, for beetles, Peasemore Wood is of more conservation interest than Hailey Wood. It is a suitable habitat for some beetle species which are rare in Britain and are identified in species recovery plans that aim to increase their numbers in UK habitats. Peasemore Wood, therefore, should take priority in management and investment for beetle conservation purposes over Hailey Wood.

However, this data does not show the overall biodiversity of either of the woodlands. There may be other species of conservation importance present in Hailey Wood that have not been recorded in this study. Therefore, further work should be carried out to assess the overall biodiversity of both of these woodlands before any decisions regarding management or investment are made for either.

Task 2 Citing references and writing a bibliography

In the *Discussion* section, you may compare your results with other studies. This will require you to cite references to other reports and published material.

You will also need to list all the references that you have referred to in your report in a bibliography at the end of your report. It is important to use a standard layout for this, such as the APA System.

2.1 **Read the citation and make a note of the order in which the author, publisher, date and place of publication are written.**

> Southwood, T. R. E. (1984). *Ecological Methods with Particular Reference to the Study of Insect Populations (*2nd ed.*)* New York: Chapman and Hall.

2.2 **In scientific writing, many bibliography references will be to articles in scientific journals. Read the two citations and answer the questions.**

> Kamikubo, Y., Shimomura, T., Fujita, Y., Tabata, T., Kashiyama, T., Sakurai, T., Fukurotani, K. & Kano, M. (2013). Functional cooperation of metabotropic adenosine and glutamate receptors regulates postsynaptic plasticity in the cerebellum. *J. Neurosci., 33*(47), 18661–18671.

> Tada, M., Takeuchi, A., Hashizume, M., Kitamura, K. & Kano, M. (2014). A highly sensitive fluorescent indicator dye for calcium imaging of neural activity *in vitro* and *in vivo*. *Eur. J. Neurosci.*, Retrieved from http://www.ncbi.nlm.nih.gov/pmc/articles/PMC4232931/.

a. What do the numbers *33, 18661–18671* in the first citation refer to?

b. What abbreviations are used in the first and second citations?

c. What is the main difference between the two citations?

2.3 **Compare your answers with a partner and discuss the bibliography conventions.**

It is advisable to start your *Bibliography* with full details and in the correct format as soon as you start reading references, then you can add references to your list as you go along. In this way, you will find that you avoid omissions and errors, and will save yourself time.

To help you do this, always keep a detailed record of your references, for example, in a Word document.

When you have finished the report, give your *Bibliography* a final check, making sure it is complete and presented in the correct format.

Task 3 What to include in the *Introduction*

Now that you have written the *Materials and Methods*, *Results* and *Discussion* sections, you are in a position to write an *Introduction* to your report.

3.1   What questions do you answer in the *Introduction* section of your report?

_____

_____

3.2   Read the statements about the *Introduction* and decide which ones are true (T) or false (F).

a.   An *Introduction* describes when an experiment was done.   ☐

b.   An *Introduction* describes the results of the investigation.   ☐

c.   The *Introduction* describes the background of your experiment.   ☐

d.   The *Introduction* describes the aim of your experiment.   ☐

e.   The *Introduction* identifies unexpected results.   ☐

3.3   Read the example of an *Introduction* and number the paragraphs in the correct order.

Beetles in Woodland Habitats

Introduction

☐   Many of these species are the subject of species recovery plans designed to manage suitable habitat and increase their numbers. Organisations with responsibilities for areas of woodlands are often lacking in sufficient resources to protect the entire woodland habitat under their jurisdiction.

☐   Woodland habitats have been in decline throughout Britain for centuries. This decline has been most notable since the Industrial Revolution and the mechanization of farming practices.

☐   Therefore, they have to prioritise woodlands that are in need of immediate protection.

☐   The organisms under most threat are the plants and the insects. These organisms tend to have low dispersal rates and are slow to colonise new habitats. Many species of plants and invertebrates are now threatened with extinction in Britain due to a loss of habitat.

☐   With the decline in woodland, many organisms are under threat from a loss of habitat.

☐   This study assesses the importance of two woodland habitats to beetle conservation.

Task 4 What makes a good *Title*?

The *Title* gives the reader a concise and informative description of the focus of your report. It summarises the information contained in the *Introduction* and *Results* sections. You may use a 'working title' during the writing stages, but you should revise it when your report is complete.

The title should give the reader a complete description of the study and include important keywords and phrases.

4.1   Read the titles. Work in groups to decide which one is better, and why.

a.   Determination of metabolic rate.

b.   The effect of temperature on oxygen consumption in mice.

4.2   Discuss your findings as a class.

4.3   Work with a partner to compare the two pairs of titles. Think about the different information each pair gives the reader. Come to a clear conclusion about the importance of an appropriate title.

a.   1. Species composition of summer phytoplankton in Lake Windermere, Great Britain
     2. Sampling plankton in a lake

b.   1. Effects of pollutants on Daphnia
     2. Morphological and ultrastructural effects of sublethal cadmium poisoning on Daphnia species

Reflect

Review the scientific report template you constructed at the end of Unit 1.
List important features you should include under each section of your template.

At the end of this unit, you will:

- understand how to check your work for grammatical and vocabulary mistakes
- practise editing your work to ensure that you use full sentences that are clear and concise

Task 1 What do I check for?

After you have written your report, it is important to check for mistakes and errors. You must allow time for this vital aspect of preparing a good report.

You will get into the habit of editing more efficiently if you are aware of the key areas in which you tend to make mistakes.

The high temperature ^{sp} effected the results.

1.1 How good are your skills in editing and revising a report? Evaluate your current skills by completing the questionnaire. Mark your competence in each skill on a scale of 1 to 5 (1 = poor, 5 = excellent). Compare your marks with a partner.

skill	score
Organising my time to allow for editing and revising a report	
Spelling of general vocabulary	
Using specialist vocabulary	
Spelling of specialist vocabulary	
Applying correct numbering conventions	
Using abbreviations correctly	
Using punctuation to help the reader	
Writing clearly and concisely	
Spotting grammatical errors, for example, in use of tenses	
Writing well-constructed sentences	
Writing well-constructed paragraphs	

1.2 As you work through this unit, you will have the opportunity to improve the areas that you find most difficult. Can you think of any other problem areas you should check when you revise and edit a report?

- _____
- _____
- _____
- _____
- _____

6

Task 2 Use of tenses

In this module, you have looked at the academic conventions for use of different tenses and aspects in scientific reports. It is important to remember to use these correctly and consistently in your work.

2.1 **The table shows sections and topics that might be included in a scientific report. For each one, decide whether the past or present tense should be used in the example sentence by circling the correct option.**

section of report	example sentence
a. The *Materials and Methods* section	The apparatus *is / was* set up as shown.
b. Referring to a table or graph	Table 1 *presents / presented* the results from sites 3 and 4.
c. Stating (quoting) the findings of published work	Cadmium *is / was* a highly toxic metal to freshwater fish (Ball, 1999).
d. The *Results* section	Oxygen production *varies / varied* depending on the pH of the solution.
e. Referring to someone else's work	Smith (2002) *finds / found* that …
f. To make a general statement	Respiration *is / was* a complex series of chemical reactions that *results / resulted* in the release of energy from food.

2.2 **Identify any sentence(s) which use the passive voice. Work with a partner to discuss why you think it should be used.**

Task 3 Common mistakes with vocabulary

The following exercise identifies some words that are commonly confused in scientific writing.

3.1 **Read the pairs of sentences. Choose the correct word to complete each sentence.**
   a. *affect / effect*
      1. Temperature strongly _____ the rate of reaction.
      2. The study investigated the _____ of temperature on rate of reaction.
   b. *continual / continuous*
      1. The tank was provided with a _____ supply of nitrogen.
      2. Impurities can be eliminated by _____ heating, cooling and reheating.
   c. *site / cite*
      1. Smith's study _____ several previous incidents.
      2. The _____ chosen for the experiment was a nearby pond.
   d. *their / there*
      1. _____ is more than one way to do this.
      2. The crabs were fed daily and _____ food supply was adjusted gradually.

3.2 **Write sentences of your own for each of the following pairs of words. Use a standard dictionary to check the meaning and spelling of terms.**

   a. *fewer / less*

   b. *breath / breathe*

   c. *rise / raise*

   d. *consecutive / concurrent*

3.3 **Compare your ideas with a partner's.**

Task 4 Plurals

Scientific words often have irregular plurals, particularly if they come from Greek or Latin terms. You will need to notice and remember common patterns, such as those in the table below.

You should also check that you are consistent in your use of plural nouns, and that plural subjects agree with the verb that follows them.

4.1 **Complete the table of singulars and plurals of common scientific terms.**

singular	plural
analysis	
	bacteria
	criteria
datum	
formula	
hypothesis	
medium	
ratio	
	phenomena

4.2 **Complete the sentences.**

   a. Greek- or Latin-based singular nouns that end in ~*um* generally form the plural by changing _____.

   b. Greek- or Latin-based singular nouns that end in ~*is* generally form the plural by changing _____.

4.3 **Decide whether the subjects and verbs agree in the sentences. Correct them if necessary.**

   a. This data is supported by evidence from other studies.

       _____

   b. Ten drops of hydrochloric acid were added to each sample.

       _____

   c. The periods of immersion for crabs at different times of the tidal cycle are presented in Table 1.

       _____

   d. One source of error in these experiments are the inaccuracy in recording light intensities.

       _____

Task 5 Be clear and concise

When writing reports, it is important to consider your audience. Unless you take great care to write clearly, it is easy to confuse the reader, particularly if you are describing a complex experiment or set of results. One way to ensure clarity is to make sure that you do not use more words than necessary.

5.1 **Work with a partner or in small groups to discuss how you would revise the sentences to eliminate unnecessary words.**

> In the experiment, the test animals were subject to analysis for investigation of their gut contents.
>
> *The gut contents of the test animals were analysed.*

a. One of the environmental conditions to which the zooplankton were shown to be affected by was pH.

b. The experiments alone are insufficient to tell what the optimum conditions are.

c. Ten test tubes were labelled with the following concentrations of sodium chloride and 50 ml of those solutions were then prepared and placed in the test tubes: 0%, 5%, 10%, 15%, 20%, 25%, 30%, 35%, 40%, 45%.

Task 6 Write in complete sentences

Another reason why reports are sometimes difficult to read is that they are not written using complete, well-formed sentences.

6.1 **Work with a partner to rewrite *a*, *b* and *c* to make complete, well-formed sentences. When you have written your sentences, compare them with those of other pairs.**

> In accordance with the Law of Limiting Factors, rate of photosynthesis is affected by light intensity, temperature and carbon dioxide concentration. Resulting in maximum rates in optimum conditions.
>
> *In accordance with the Law of Limiting Factors, the rate of photosynthesis is affected by light intensity, temperature and carbon dioxide concentration and maximum rates occur in optimum conditions.*

a. In the third set of experiments, citric acid concentration was doubled and at each temperature three sets of readings.

_____

_____

b. Enzymes are denatured at high temperatures. Because molecular conformation is altered.

_____

_____

c. The reaction occurred at its maximum; copper was absent.

_____

_____

Task 7 Write well-constructed paragraphs

Each section of your report should be written in well-organised paragraphs.

7.1 **Are the statements true (T) or false (F)? Discuss your answers as a class.**

a. Each paragraph presents one main point or idea. ☐

b. A paragraph starts by stating the main general point in a topic sentence, then moves onto more specific information. ☐

c. Paragraphs of text are not included in the *Results* section of your report. ☐

d. The *Materials and Methods* section of your report is written in bullet points, not paragraphs. ☐

e. Paragraphs must be arranged in a logical order. ☐

Reflect

Draw up an 'Editing checklist'. Compare your list with the one given on page 27.

Choose a scientific report you have completed recently and have a writing conference with a fellow student (peer review). Use the Editing checklist as a basis for your discussions.

Web work

Using the passive voice

http://www.grammarbank.com/passive-voice-exercises.html

Review

This site provides exercises in using the passive voice. You can check your answers and get instant feedback.

Task

Complete the exercises listed on the site.

Interpreting data (1)

http://www.admc.hct.ac.ae/hd1/english/graphs/oupgraphs.pdf

Review

This site presents exercises to test your use of verbs, adverbs and prepositions in describing graphs. The final exercise tests your skill in interpreting and describing information in a pie chart.

Interpreting data (2)

http://www.kirkfisher.com/wp-content/uploads/2012/08/Making-Science-Graphs-and-Interpreting-Data.pdf

Review

This site presents exercises in drawing graphs and interpreting data. It includes exercises on interpreting line graphs, histograms, tables and pie charts.

Interpreting data (3)

http://www.mmu.k12.vt.us/teachers/eschholz/RegBio-GraphPractice.pdf

Review

This site presents exercises in interpreting data from a table and drawing graphs.

Task

Complete the exercises on these sites.

Extension activities

Before writing your first report, it is helpful to study a few short papers in a major scientific journal, such as *Ecology, Developmental Biology* or *Genetics*. Choose papers in journals from your own field. You don't need to read for content, but look at the way in which the paper is crafted.

Answer the questions.

a. What is included in the *Introduction*?

b. How much detail is given in the *Materials and Methods* section?

c. How are the results presented in the *Results* section? If graphs are presented, how are axes labelled?

d. How are titles written for tables and figures?

e. What is included in the *Discussion*?

f. How are references cited?

When you have written the first draft of a scientific report, use the checklist to edit and revise your report.

Editing checklist

- Is the *Title* descriptive and concise?
- Does the *Introduction* include background information, supported by references from the literature?
- Does the *Introduction* include the aim of the study?
- Is the *Materials and Methods* section written in the past tense?
- Is the *Materials and Methods* section written in the passive voice where appropriate?
- Does the *Materials and Methods* section contain all the information required to repeat the experiment?
- Does the *Results* section contain tables and figures, with titles that inform and can be understood without reference to the text?
- Does the *Results* section contain text describing results with reference to each table and figure?
- Does the *Discussion* explain what the results mean?
- Does the *Discussion* compare results with those from other studies and cite references?
- Does the *Discussion* assess errors and unexpected results and suggest extensions?
- Is the *Bibliography* presented correctly?
- Are *References* cited correctly in the text?
- Is writing clear and concise?
- Are numbers, abbreviations, punctuation and spelling correct?

G

Glossary

analyse (v) To break an issue down into parts in order to study, identify and discuss their meaning and/or relevance.

Bibliography (n) A list of references to sources cited in the text of a piece of academic writing or a book. A bibliography should consist of an alphabetical list of books, papers, journal articles and websites and is usually found at the end of the work. It may also include texts suggested by the author for further reading.

checklist (n) A list of tasks to do or aspects to consider when planning and preparing for an event such as an academic assignment, journey or party.

cite (v) To acknowledge sources of ideas in your work. This may be done through an in-text reference to an author, a reference in a bibliography or footnote, or a verbal reference in a talk or lecture.

concise (adj) Used to describe something that is expressed clearly in a few well-chosen words.

Conclusion (n) In academic terms, the final part of an essay or presentation, usually involving a summary of your results or argument, and a judgement.

criteria (n) Qualities, rules or standards on which decisions or judgements are based.

deadline (n) The date or time by which something needs to be completed. In academic situations, deadlines are normally given for handing in essays and assignments.

decimal (n) (adj) 1 (n) A fraction expressed using numbers to the right of a decimal point. For example, one-quarter expressed as a decimal is 0.25. 2 (adj) Used to describe any numbering based on tens.

dependent variable (n) In an experiment or study, a variable that changes in response to the independent variable or control. For example, if the response of insects to a particular chemical is being measured, the independent variable is the amount of chemical that is administered and the dependent variable is the degree to which the insects respond.

deviation (n) A variation or movement away from a standard or expected result.

Discussion section (n) The section of a scientific paper that analyses the findings or results of an experiment.

draft (n) (v) 1 (n) An early version of a piece of academic writing that is used as the starting point for further work. 2 (v) To create an early version of an essay, knowing that you will go back afterwards to develop and edit your language and ideas.

edit (v) To select, rearrange and improve material to make it more suitable for its final purpose. Editing material involves reorganising it, correcting errors, improving the wording or content and changing its length by adding sections or taking them out.

evaluate (v) To assess information in terms of quality, relevance, objectivity and accuracy.

experiment (n) A test under controlled conditions to examine whether or not a hypothesis is true.

fieldwork (n) Research or information collected away from the classroom, office or laboratory where you usually do your work.

figure (n) A diagram, graph or picture that illustrates information in a text.

formula (n) An equation, fact or rule expressed in symbols and sometimes numbers, for example, πr^2 (pi r squared) is the formula for the area of a circle.

fraction (n) The expression of a number as part of a whole. It is shown as a quotient, where one number (the numerator) is divided by another (the denominator), such as ¼, ½ and ⅜.

histogram (n) A form of graph that uses horizontal or vertical bars. The width (when horizontal) or height (when vertical) of the bars are in proportion to the values of the data items they represent.

hypothesis (n) An idea about, or explanation of an observation, phenomenon or scientific problem. Hypotheses are tested by experimentation or analysis.

implication (n) Something that can be interpreted or inferred, but is not directly stated.

independent variable (n) The variable in an experiment or study that the investigator can control or manipulate. For example, if the response of insects to a particular chemical is being measured, the independent variable is the amount of chemical that is administered and the dependent variable is the degree to which the insects respond.

interpret (v) Give the meaning or explain the significance of something as you understand it.

keyword (n) An important word in a text. Keywords are often used as a reference point to search for other words or information.

laboratory schedule (n) A list of procedures or instructions for conducting an experiment or operation in the laboratory.

layout (n) The way that things are positioned within a space, for example, the way text, pictures and diagrams are arranged on a page or computer screen.

line graph (n) A graph that highlights trends by showing connecting lines between data points.

Materials and Methods section (n) The section of a scientific report that gives an account of the procedure that was followed in an experiment. It also details the materials and equipment that were used.

numeral (n) A symbol used to represent a number: 1, 2, 3, 4, etc., are numerals.

ordinal (n) Symbols that show the position of a numbered item in a series. For example, 1st, 2nd, 3rd and 4th.

peer review (n) The process of getting colleagues or other students to check one's work. The idea is that peers can identify each other's errors quickly and effectively.

pie chart (n) A graphic representation of amounts or percentages which are shown as segments of a circle (like a pie that has been divided up). It can be used instead of a table in the *Results* section of a scientific writing report.

plot (v) To mark points on a graph or chart.

protocol (n) Standard procedures and principles that are followed, for example, when writing a report or conducting an experiment.

quotation (n) A part of a text written or spoken by one author and reproduced in a text, piece of academic writing or talk by another author. When you quote someone's words or ideas, you do not change the wording at all and should put them in inverted commas to signal that it is a quotation.

ratio (n) The relation between two quantities expressed as the quotient of one divided by the other. For example, the ratio of 9 to 4 is 9:4 or 9/4.

reference (n) (v) 1 (n) Acknowledgment of the sources of ideas and information that you use in written work and oral presentations. 2 (v) To acknowledge or mention sources of information.

research (n) (v) 1 (n) Information collected from a variety of sources about a specific topic. 2 (v) To gather information from a variety of sources and analyse and compare it.

scale (n) A sequence of marks at fixed intervals used to show measurements on, for example, a ruler, graph or map.

source (n) Something (usually a book, article or other text) that supplies you with information. In an academic context, sources used in essays and reports must be acknowledged.

theoretical background (n) Academic ideas and information that must be studied and understood before conducting an experiment, and that should be considered and referred to in the discussion stage of a scientific report.

trend (n) The general direction in which something moves, or a sudden change in direction.

Notes

Notes

Published by
Garnet Publishing Ltd.
8 Southern Court
South Street
Reading RG1 4QS, UK

This book is based on an original concept devised by Dr Anthony Manning and Mrs Frances Russell.

ISBN 978 1 78260 180 7

British Library Cataloguing-in-Publication Data
A catalogue record for this book is available from the British Library.

Production
Project manager: Clare Chandler
Editorial team: Clare Chandler, Matthew George,
                     Sophia Hopton, Martin Moore
Design & Layout: Madeleine Maddock
Photography: iStockphoto, Shutterstock

Garnet Publishing and the authors of TASK would like to thank the staff and students of the International Foundation Programme at the University of Reading for their respective roles in the development of these teaching materials.

Garnet Publishing would like to thank Jane Brooks and Ray de Witt for their contribution to the First edition of the TASK series.

All website URLs provided in this publication were correct at the time of printing. If any URL does not work, please contact your tutor, who will help you find similar resources.

Printed and bound in Lebanon by International Press: interpress@int-press.com

Acknowledgements
Page 13:   Task 1, Guidelines for writing numbers, taken from, Council of Science Editors, Style Manual Subcommittee. (2014) *Scientific Style and Format: The CSE Manual for Authors, Editors, and Publishers.* (8th ed.). Chicago (IL): University of Chicago Press. Reproduced with permission.